POST MORTEM

A R Gurney

REFERENC

Form 178 re

D1264221

BROADWAY PLAY PUBLISHING INC
56 E 81st St., NY NY 10028-0202
212 772-8334 fax: 212 772-8358
BroadwayPlayPubl.com

First printing: December 2006
I S B N: 0-88145-328-5

Book design: Marie Donovan
Word processing: Microsoft Word
Typographic controls: Ventura Publisher
Typeface: Palatino
Printed and bound in the U S A

ABOUT THE AUTHOR

A R ("Pete") Gurney's work has been produced in New York at Lincoln Center, Manhattan Theater Club, Playwrights Horizons, and Primary Stages. Among his plays are THE DINING ROOM, THE COCKTAIL HOUR, LOVE LETTERS, SYLVIA, FAR EAST, THE FOURTH WALL, and BIG BILL. More recently, three of his more political plays—O JERUSALEM, MRS FARNSWORTH, and SCREEN PLAY—have been produced at the Flea Theater in Tribeca. Gurney has also written several published novels, as well as the libretto for Michael Torkes opera *Strawberry Fields*, presented by the New York City Opera. A former Professor of Literature at M I T, he was elected in 2005 to the Theater Hall of Fame, and in 2006 to The American Academy of Arts and Letters. He lives in Connecticut with his wife Molly, where they welcome their large family.

POST MORTEN play was first produced at the
Flea Theatre in New York City (Jim Simpson,
Artistic Director; Carol Ostrow, Producing Director),
opening on 2 November 2006. The cast and creative
contributors were:

ALICE .... Tina Benko
DEXTER .... Christopher Kromer
BETSY .... Shannon Burkett

Director .... Jim Simpson
Set design .... Mimi Lien
Lighting design ....Brian Aldous
Costume design .... Claudia Brown
Production stage manager ....Jennifer Noterman

CHARACTERS & SETTING

ALICE, *a lecturer in drama at a faith-based state university in the Mid-West*

DEXTER, *a senior at the same university.*

BETSY, *a student at this university, later on in time.*

ALICE's *office: A bookcase with books; a desk with papers and folders on it; a couple of chairs.*

Later, an open stage: three chairs and a low table.

Time: Sometime in the future.

for Carol Ostrow
with great appreciation

(At rise)

*(*ALICE *is at her desk, reading a worn old paperback. .She is an attractive youngish woman. She acts out what she reads silently, becoming more and more melodramatic, even as she occasionally glances out the door and steals an occasional glance at her watch. Soon she is mouthing the words; then speaking them aloud. Finally she tosses aside the book, and acts out the speech with full fervor.)*

ALICE: *(With a Southern accent)* "...Maybe we are a long way from being made in God's image, but Stella— my sister—there has been *some* progress since then! Such things as art—as poetry and music—such kinds of new light have come into the world... In some kinds of people some tenderer feelings have had some little beginning! That we have got to make *grow!* And *cling* to, and hold as our flag! In this dark march toward whatever it is we're approaching... *Don't hang back with the brutes!"*

(During her speech, DEXTER *appears in the doorway. He is in his twenties, scruffily dressed, probably in a flannel hoodie, though he also wears a loosely tied necktie. He stands and listens.)*

DEXTER: *(Applauding at the end of the speech)* Cool.

ALICE: *(Startled)* You heard all that?

DEXTER: Most of it.

ALICE: That's called eavesdropping.

DEXTER: Couldn't help it. You're good!

ALICE: Tennessee Williams is good.

DEXTER: Who?

ALICE: Tennessee Williams. I've mentioned him in class.

DEXTER: Oh yeah, him.

ALICE: A major American playwright.

DEXTER: You make him sound terrific.

ALICE: Thank you. I wanted to be an actor, back in high school.

DEXTER: Why did you give it up?

ALICE: I didn't. The school cancelled the drama program. And our local community theatre withered away. There wasn't much opportunity to get on a stage.

DEXTER: So you decided to teach instead.

ALICE: At least it gives me an audience. And a chance to sound off.

DEXTER: You should do that speech in class.

ALICE: Tennessee Williams? A homosexual playwright? Who wrote about rape, castration, and murder? You want me to perform him out *loud*? Here? In a border state? At a faith-based university, supported by public funds?

DEXTER: Take it easy.

ALICE: Well I mean get serious.

DEXTER: I hear you.

ALICE: We are allowed to read silently, and refer to occasionally, certain writers like Tennessee Williams, but we're asking for trouble to go much beyond that.

DEXTER: O K, O K.

ALICE: *(Putting the book away)* You're late for your appointment, by the way.

DEXTER: It took longer than I thought to get through security.

ALICE: This is a tough building.

DEXTER: Tell me about it.

ALICE: They think because we teach the Humanities, we're potential subversives.

DEXTER: Are they right?

ALICE: *(Loudly, pointing towards a light fixture towards the ceiling)* No, no!. Of course not.

DEXTER: *(Whispering; pointing up)* Don't tell me we're bugged.

ALICE: There's a rumor to that effect.

DEXTER: *(Softly)* I hear they're bugged in Political Science.

ALICE: *(Loudly)* I know nothing about Political Science. *(More softly)* No, dammit. I'm going to assume we're not bugged. Just because the administration is paranoid , it doesn't mean we have to be.... Did security make you take off your clothes?

DEXTER: Not this time.

ALICE: You're lucky.

DEXTER: Don't tell me they make you?

ALICE: Depends who's monitoring...

DEXTER: If I were a monitor, I might make you.

ALICE: Stop right there.

DEXTER: It just slipped out.

ALICE: Well, put it back in.

DEXTER: I'll try.

ALICE: I'm serious now.

DEXTER: O K, O K... I can't believe they'd check out a member of the faculty.

ALICE: I'm a lowly lecturer. I don't count....

DEXTER: Do you have to carry a Bible around?

ALICE: Oh sure. Even full Professors have to do that. *(She indicates the Bible displayed on her desk.)*

DEXTER: That's really why I was late. I forgot my Bible. I had to go into the Memorization Room and learn something from the Psalms.

ALICE: Did they make you recite it?

DEXTER: "I will lift up mine eyes unto the hills, from whence cometh my help."

ALICE: *(Joining him)* "My help cometh from the Lord who hath made heaven and earth."

DEXTER: Not many hills around here.

ALICE: No, it's very...flat. So our help has to cometh from somewhere else.

DEXTER: Like where?

ALICE: Books. Plays. Literature... But don't get me started. *(Goes to book case to get his folder)* Why did you make this appointment?

DEXTER: I want to do my senior thesis with you.

ALICE: No.

DEXTER: Why no?

ALICE: I'm not impressed with your commitment to the drama.

DEXTER: What? I've taken three of your courses!

ALICE: *(As she checks his folder)* Yes, but you barely passed any of them. Your written work was totally sub-standard. And your classroom participation negligible.

DEXTER: That's because I was distracted.

ALICE: By what?

DEXTER: You.

ALICE: Now back off! I mean that!

DEXTER: Sorry.

ALICE: Where have you been, by the way? I haven't seen you around .

DEXTER: I took last semester off.

ALICE: Financial problems?

DEXTER: Personal problems.

ALICE: I'm sorry.

DEXTER: Want to know what the problem was?

ALICE: Well, I don't suppose it's any of my—

DEXTER: You. You were the problem.

ALICE: Oh please.

DEXTER: I left school to get away from you. But now I've decided to come back.

ALICE: What changed your mind?

DEXTER: I found a topic.

ALICE: A topic?

DEXTER: For my senior thesis. Something to work on. With you.

ALICE: Not on your life.

DEXTER: Seriously. I'm ready to concentrate big-time.

ALICE: Sorry. I've got too much on my plate already. I'm working on several other senior projects. That's more than enough overtime for a lowly lecturer who's supposed to be writing a book.

DEXTER: You could write that book with me.

ALICE: No thanks.

DEXTER: I've got an extremely exciting topic.

ALICE: I've already turned down plenty of exciting topics—including one on Tennessee Williams.

DEXTER: Mine's way beyond that.

ALICE: Now look, my friend...

DEXTER: Call me Dexter, please.

ALICE: All right. Now look, Dexter—

DEXTER: May I call you Alice?

ALICE: No.

DEXTER: Come on.

ALICE: I said no.

DEXTER: It's such a pretty name, Alice.

ALICE: All *right*! Call me whatever you want, but it's still no go.

DEXTER: You haven't even heard my topic.

ALICE: Name it.

(*Pause*)

DEXTER: Now I'm embarrassed.

ALICE: Why?

DEXTER: I'm scared you'll laugh..

ALICE: Why would I laugh?

DEXTER: It's so unusual.

ALICE: I'm waiting.

(Pause)

DEXTER: Gurney.

ALICE: Who?

DEXTER: Gurney. A R Gurney.

ALICE: You've lost me, Dexter.

DEXTER: I want to work on Gurney.

ALICE: You're saying someone named Gurney wrote plays?

DEXTER: Right.

ALICE: Excuse me, please. *(Opens her lap-top)* While I look him up.

DEXTER: *(Quickly)* Don't!

ALICE: What?

DEXTER: Does the university monitor you when you go on the internet?

ALICE: Of course.

DEXTER: Then for God's sake don't google Gurney.

ALICE: Don't google Gurney?

DEXTER: He's too dangerous.

ALICE: Oh come on.

DEXTER: Trust me.

ALICE: *(Going to book-case)* Then I'll lift up my eyes unto a book.. *(Takes out a large reference book, shows it to him)* "Brief Biographies in World Theatre" ... *(Looks in index)* Gurney, you say? ...Is that G-U or G-U-E?

DEXTER: Just G-U.

ALICE: *(Putting down book)* Nope. Nothing here.

DEXTER: You're sure?

ALICE: *(Putting book back)* There's a Guare there. No Gurney.

DEXTER: Shit.

ALICE: *(Gets out another book)* Let's try another source. *(Reads title) Minor Figures in American Drama*

DEXTER: He should definitely be there.

ALICE: *(Thumbing through, finding it)* Eureka! Here he is.

DEXTER: Yippee. Yay.

ALICE: A small squib. *(Reads)* "A R Gurney...middle class comedies of manners..." *(To* DEXTER*)* I take it this is your man.

DEXTER: That's my man.

ALICE: This is the playwright who brought you back to school?

DEXTER: This is the playwright who brought me back to you.

ALICE: This is the playwright on whom you intend to focus a substantial part of the second term of your senior year? In spite of all the great playwrights in history? Sophocles...Shakespeare...Ibsen...

DEXTER: I still pick Gurney.

ALICE: Forgive me, but I have to ask why?

DEXTER: Because of what he wrote.

ALICE: You've read his work?

DEXTER: All of it.

ALICE: And you've found things?

DEXTER: Major things.

ALICE: *(Thumbing through book)* There's very little on him here. *(Reading)* It seems he led a boring, *bourgeois* life.

DEXTER: That's wrong.

ALICE: How do you know it's wrong?

DEXTER: I found his privately printed autobiography in a used book store.

ALICE: You've actually done research!

DEXTER: All last semester.

ALICE: Good for you, Dexter.

DEXTER: Thanks, Alice.

ALICE: And what did his autobiography tell you?

DEXTER: He had a series of affairs with various movie actresses.

ALICE: Oh really? I happen to be familiar with the stars of that period. Did he mention names?

DEXTER: He mentioned Hepburn.

ALICE: Audrey or Katharine?

DEXTER: Both.

ALICE: Gurney had affairs with both Hepburns?

DEXTER: He also mentions an actress named Cameron Diaz.

ALICE: He had an affair with her, too?

DEXTER: She was nuts about him, according to his memoir.

ALICE: These private memoirs aren't always trustworthy, Dexter.

DEXTER: I'm aware of that, Alice.

ALICE: Besides, sexual conquests don't necessarily make Gurney a better playwright. By his works shall ye know him.

DEXTER: That's why I turned to his plays.

ALICE: When did he live? *(She starts to look it up in her book)*

DEXTER: He was born in 1930.

ALICE: So he was primarily a Twentieth Century playwright.

DEXTER: Primarily, yes. But he continued writing on into the Twenty-First.

ALICE: When he was what? Over seventy?

DEXTER: Right.

ALICE: Shakespeare retired when he was fifty.

DEXTER: Thank God Gurney didn't.

ALICE: Maybe he should have.

DEXTER: You won't say that when you read his stuff.

ALICE: You mean that this Gurney person had something special to tell us, even in his declining years?

DEXTER: Absolutely.

ALICE: *(Going to coffee maker)* I might have a cup of coffee. Will you join me?

DEXTER: Nope. I'm too wound up as it is.

ALICE: About Gurney?

DEXTER: About you.

ALICE: I've repeatedly asked you to knock that off.

DEXTER: I'm trying.

ALICE: Try harder, please. *(Fussing with coffee)* You might tell me what put you onto this fellow? How did you discover he even existed?

DEXTER: I was poking around in the library last spring, before I quit school, and there he was.

ALICE: In the library? *Our* library? After the last purge?
I thought you said he was a dangerous writer.

DEXTER: Oh he's not in the stacks. He's hidden in
the cellar, next to some bound copies of the old Time
Magazine. I'm a huge Red Sox fan, so I was looking up
an article on Ted Williams, when I happened to notice a
couple of Gurney's plays. So I glanced through them.

ALICE: And they grabbed you?

DEXTER: Not really. But I discovered we had something
very much in common.

ALICE: And what, pray tell, was that?

DEXTER: Politics.

ALICE: I find that interesting.

DEXTER: I figured you would.

ALICE: Why do you say that?

DEXTER: Because I noticed in class that you also got
hung up on the same thing.

ALICE: *(Glancing toward the ceiling)* Hung up?

DEXTER: You kept bringing up where we are politically...

ALICE: *(Loudly, as if to the possible listening device)*
Everyone has political concerns, Dexter. According
to Aristotle, man is a political animal.

DEXTER: In some of your classroom comments, I noticed
you got quite specific. You talked about what happened
to our country at the turn of the Twenty-First Century.

ALICE: *(Indicating office door)* Is there someone out there?

(DEXTER *gets up, looks out into the hall)*

DEXTER: No.

ALICE: I thought I saw a shadow.

DEXTER: I didn't.

ALICE: I wish I could close that door.

DEXTER: Why don't you?

ALICE: It's against the rules. "Doors are to remain open during office hours."

DEXTER: That's because of sexual harassment issues

ALICE: Oh is that it?

DEXTER: I can understand that, Alice. I could easily harass you, if that door were closed.

ALICE: I'll ignore that remark.

DEXTER: Well it's true.

ALICE: I believe that they want our doors open to discourage people from talking about politics. But there I go, getting paranoid again. Professor Watson over in History tells me he has been able to teach Franklin Roosevelt and the New Deal without even a reprimand. *(Glancing up)* I'm just used to being, well, careful, that's all. *(Giving her rotating desk a chair a little spin)* But I have to say, Dexter, that for some reason, with you here, I feel slightly rebellious.

DEXTER: I'm glad I have that effect, Alice.

ALICE: So tell me more about...why do I keep forgetting his name?

DEXTER: Gurney.

ALICE: Tell me about his politics.

DEXTER: He wrote several plays with political themes.

ALICE: I'm amazed they're in our library.

DEXTER: They're not.

ALICE: You said they were in the cellar.

DEXTER: Not the political plays. What I found in the cellar were good-humored, easy-going comedies obviously written earlier. The political plays were produced later on, at a delightful little theatre in the Tribeca area of New York City. Only a few copies escaped confiscation. I tracked them down last fall.

ALICE: Good for you! You're beginning to show some enterprise, Dexter..

DEXTER: I'm strongly motivated, Alice.

ALICE: *(Going to bookcase)* I have a book somewhere... a book of drama criticism...they had critics for plays then, rather than censors , by the way.

DEXTER: Oh yeah?

ALICE: *(As she looks for a book)* Oh yes. Playwrights could write whatever they wanted, but there were these critics who criticized them.

DEXTER: Sounds cool.

ALICE: Cool? Yes, I suppose it was "cool", if the critics liked you. If they didn't, it could be quite disheartening. Especially since one critic from one newspaper pretty much determined your fate.

DEXTER: Hey. No fair.

ALICE: I know, but that's the way it was. And no one did much about it.

DEXTER: At least you could get up to bat—even if you struck out.

ALICE: Good point. *(Finds the book)* Ah. Here's the book of criticism. Let's see if anyone says anything about your man Gurney... *(Looks through book)* We'll see, we'll see.... Hmmm... There's only one entry.... Here it is. *(Reads)* "...a large part of Gurney's life was spent teaching. As a result, many of his plays have to do with teachers and students."

(They look at each other)

DEXTER: That's true enough.

ALICE: *(Continuing)* "As a result, a faint layer of chalk dust settles over much of his work, along with a kind of chuckly, professorial tone. As a result, Gurney can be not only disappointing, but sometimes downright annoying." *(To DEXTER)* Did you find that also "true enough"?

DEXTER: Sometimes.

ALICE: Even in his political plays?

DEXTER: Yep. Even there.

ALICE: Hmmm. Well, Dexter. Let me say that despite your good efforts, I am still underwhelmed by your project. *(Checks her watch; jumps up)* Woops. It's time for my seminar on Chekhov. No chalk dust settling over that good gentleman, I hasten to add.

DEXTER: What do I do about my thesis?

ALICE: Try someone else in the department.

DEXTER: But I want you.

ALICE: I'm sorry. You've told me some mildly interesting things, but on balance, I have to say Gurney doesn't light any fires in me. And I need to feel fire.... *(A glance at the ceiling; more softly)* ...especially in these dark and philistine times. *(Starts out)*

DEXTER: Alice.

ALICE: What?

DEXTER: Do I light any fires in you?

ALICE: Of course not.

DEXTER: You light fires in me. Fires I'm finding it difficult to put out.

ALICE: You're barking up the wrong tree, Dexter.

DEXTER: I don't consider you a tree, Alice. Or if you mean that metaphorically, I consider you lone of Robert Frost's birches, on which I'd like to swing forever.

ALICE: Oh please. *(Starts out again)*

DEXTER: Wait!

ALICE: What now?

DEXTER: I haven't told you my special angle on Gurney.

ALICE: You've told me more than enough.

DEXTER: I've avoided mentioning the really exciting point.

ALICE: *(Checking her watch)* I'll be late for class.

DEXTER: But this could really knock the socks off you.

ALICE: Put it in writing, leave it on my desk and I'll consider it when I get back, *(Starts out again)*

DEXTER: I don't dare put it in writing.

ALICE: *(Stopping again)* Don't dare?

DEXTER: Someone might see it, and steal my thunder.

ALICE: You have something thunderous to say about A J Gurney?

DEXTER: A R Gurney...I believe I do. Yes.

ALICE: Suppose you wait here while I teach my class. Feel free to browse among my books. I'll be back in an hour.

(She goes out. DEXTER waits expectantly. After a long moment, ALICE hurries back in)

ALICE: *(Striding past him to her desk)* Oh for God's sake, Dexter! How can I possibly go teach Chekhov, who fought so passionately against melodrama, when you suddenly dangle this melodramatic hook right under my nose?

DEXTER: I wanted to.

ALICE: I know you did. If you pulled this on some actress right before she went on stage, you'd be banished from the theatre forever. So give me your so-called "angle" quickly so I can meet my class.

DEXTER: O K. Here's the deal. I have reason to believe... *(Goes to door, looks out, looks at ceiling, then speaks furtively)* I have reason to believe that A R Gurney was murdered.

ALICE: Murdered?

DEXTER: Assassinated.

ALICE: For what cause?

DEXTER: For what he wrote.

ALICE: You mean, for his plays?

DEXTER: I mean for his last play. The one he wrote right before he was murdered.

ALICE: And what play was that?

DEXTER: It was a play called POST MORTEM.

ALICE: POST MORTEM?

DEXTER: It means "After Death".

ALICE: I know what POST MORTEM means. Dexter.

DEXTER: In this case, the title works both ways. It refers to the death of this country, or at least the death of the country Gurney once knew and loved. It also may refer to his own demise.

ALICE: How is it that the world knows nothing about this play or its title?

DEXTER: Because it wasn't published or produced.

ALICE: Why not?

DEXTER: It was too dangerous.

ALICE: And you think Gurney was murdered because of it.

DEXTER: That's what I think.

ALICE: Wait a minute. *(She to her desk, picks up reference book)* I'm returning now to my sources. *(Finds her place)* Here we are. *(Reads, looks up)* It says nothing about Gurney's death.

DEXTER: Of course it wouldn't.

ALICE: Why wouldn't it?

DEXTER: I'll let you answer that.

(Pause. She glances at the ceiling)

ALICE: So what makes you think Gurney was murdered?

DEXTER: During my semester off, I took a trip.

ALICE: A trip

DEXTER: I went to Buffalo.

ALICE: Buffalo, New York?

DEXTER: Where Gurney was born.

ALICE: You actually went there?

DEXTER: Some people do, you know.

ALICE: I'm impressed.

DEXTER: I wanted to look up his obituary in the Erie County Library.

ALICE: Did it say he was murdered?

DEXTER: Not exactly.

ALICE: What did it say?

DEXTER: It said he died in automobile accident, when his S U V smashed into an American elm on the Buffalo exit ramp of the New York Thruway.

ALICE: That sounds...possible.

DEXTER: Does it, Alice? Does it? When in several of
his plays Gurney railed against S U Vs as extravagant,
gas-guzzling monsters? In one play, he writes that he
wouldn't be caught dead in one.

ALICE: Sounds like he was.

DEXTER: Was he, Alice? There's another odd
inconsistency in that obituary. Namely, that there
is no American elm anywhere near the Buffalo exit
on the Thruway. In fact there is no American elm
anywhere in Buffalo. That lovely tree has become
completely extinct throughout the Erie basin, as
Gurney himself bemoans in one of his plays.

ALICE: How strange... But what did other obituaries say?

DEXTER: I couldn't find any other obituaries.

ALICE: But surely his death must have been mentioned
somewhere else.

DEXTER: Not if the information was suppressed.

ALICE: Suppressed? By whom?

DEXTER: Again, I'll let you answer that.

(They both glance at the ceiling, speak more softly)

ALICE: Couldn't Gurney have been the victim of some
random provincial violence?

DEXTER: Random? Maybe not. Provincial,
maybe—depending on how you view Buffalo.

ALICE: Oh I don't know, Dexter. What could possibly be
the motivation for killing a second-tier playwright at a
time when the American theatre itself was very much
on the wane?

DEXTER: I think Gurney was killed to prevent his last and greatest play from having a production, or even a staged reading.

ALICE: Was it that powerful a play?

DEXTER: It could have turned the world upside down.

ALICE: How do you know?

DEXTER: Because I've read it.

ALICE: You've read this last, lost work?

DEXTER: I've read it, studied it, even memorized parts of it.

ALICE: Memorized?

DEXTER: I've got a great memory for baseball statistics. I just reapplied that talent to Gurney's play.

ALICE: But how did you get a hold of it?

DEXTER: Ah, but you have your seminar on Chekhov.

ALICE: Do I? *(Goes to desk, picks up telephone, dials a three digits)* Mrs Sanchez? Please go to Building 14, room 307, and tell my class I'm running a little late. Ask them to write a short in-class essay on ... *(Thinks)* Evangelical Comedy. *(Into telephone)* Gracias, Mrs Sanchez... *(Hangs up, turns to* DEXTER*)* Now, Dexter. Tell me how you found this lost masterpiece.

DEXTER: I came across a cache of Gurney's possessions.

ALICE: A cache?

DEXTER: A cache is a place of concealment.

ALICE: I know what a cache is, Dexter. Go on.

DEXTER: When I became interested in the guy, I decided to locate members of his family, so I could check out letters and photographs and that stuff. I discovered that Gurney had a large family which, like most liberal families, had emigrated to Canada. But when I googled the Mormon genealogical registry in Salt Lake City, Utah, and discovered that one of his grandchildren had remained behind in Buffalo. Hey, it was like discovering that a descendant of Shakespeare's was alive and well, and living in Stratford!

ALICE: Forgive me, Dexter, but that analogy is just a tad far-fetched.

DEXTER: Put it down to my scholarly enthusiasm, Alice. And my passionate feelings towards you, personally.

ALICE: Enough, please. Go on.

DEXTER: So I telephoned this Gurney grandson—who shall remain nameless for his own safety—and asked him if he had inherited anything of his grandfather's. He said he had a few pieces of memorabilia. So I went back to Buffalo to take a look.

ALICE: Buffalo revisited...

DEXTER: Or what used to be Buffalo. The Queen City of the Great Lakes has gone back to its baser beginnings. It's now a pathetic little trading post on the Niagara River, specializing in drugs coming in and refugees going out.

ALICE: Resume your main narrative, please.

DEXTER: Right. Well, this Gurney relative was extremely friendly.. He met me at the airport, drove me to his home, and gave me a dry martini.

ALICE: A dry what?

DEXTER: Martini. It's a kind of drink. He said it was the favorite cocktail of the people his grandfather used to write about. I cautioned him not to stereotype any group, even a totally obsolete one.

ALICE: Good for you, Dexter.

DEXTER: I mean, think what our government once did to Arab-Americans.

ALICE: Good point, Dexter. Now go on.

DEXTER: Anyway after the martini and a good dinner, the grandson ushered me up to his attic where he showed me a steamer trunk.

ALICE: I assume you mean those trunks once used for travel abroad on steamships.

DEXTER: That's it. I noticed that this trunk was plastered with old ship's labels: the Mauretania, the Queen Elizabeth Two, the Carnival Cruise Line.

ALICE: There's a sense of decline and decay even in that catalogue of ships.

DEXTER: This old trunk had apparently belonged to the Gurney family for years. So I began to rummage through it while my host went downstairs to help his wife clean up after dinner.

ALICE: What did you find in that steamer trunk?

DEXTER: Oh, the first layer was the usual theatre stuff—stagey black-and-white photographs of various Gurney productions, gushy opening-night cards from actors, a number of decidedly mixed reviews from *The New YorkTimes*.

ALICE: That's all?

DEXTER: God no. At the very bottom, I discovered a large, sealed manila envelope, with the word POST MORTEM on it.

ALICE: Gurney's last play!

DEXTER: Naturally I opened it immediately. And found everything I could have wished for. *(Opening his backpack)* Let me show you.

ALICE: Don't tell me you have it with you!

DEXTER: *(Removing a large manila envelope)* I didn't dare let it out of my sight.

ALICE: You stole it? While your host was loading the dishwashing machine?

DEXTER: Shit, no! I rushed downstairs and asked if I could borrow it.

ALICE: And he agreed? He allowed this valuable material to leave the house in the hands of some visiting student?

DEXTER: I think he felt—like you, Alice—that his grandfather's work wasn't terribly important.

ALICE: *(A little sheepishly)* Still...

DEXTER: And I promised him, if anything came of it, I would give him and his family an eleven percent royalty, minus my finder's fee and travel expenses.

ALICE: Didn't our guards notice the play today, when you came through security?

DEXTER: I told them it was just a screenplay I was working on. As you know, everyone carries around one of those.

ALICE: You have all the answers, don't you, Dexter?

DEXTER: No I don't, Alice, but perhaps this manuscript does.... *(Opens it, holds up a black manuscript, then slams it down on her desk)* If this were a poker game, I'd say read it and weep.

ALICE: *(Reaching for it)* I certainly intend to.

DEXTER: *(Taking it up again)* But not yet. *(Takes three documents out of the covering envelope)* Before you do, I think you should read what was attached to the script. *(Handing her an e-mail print out)* First: This e-mail letter addressed to Gurney from his agent.

ALICE: *(Taking, reading the document)* "Dear Pete..." *(Looking up)* Why "Pete"?

DEXTER: Apparently it was a nickname. According to his grandson, the only people who ever called him "Albert" were insurance salesmen and fund-raisers for public television..

ALICE: They say public television used to be wonderful!

DEXTER: Not when they were fund-raising.

ALICE: *(Reading more)* "Dear Pete: I have just finished reading your wonderful new play POST MORTEM. It makes me proud to be your agent. I believe it will turn out to be one of the great plays of this, or any other, century."

DEXTER: You see?

ALICE: Wait. He goes on. *(Reads)* "Therefore I recommend that you immediately turn it into a musical." *(Perplexed)* What else should I read?

DEXTER: *(Hands her a hand-written note)* This is a woman's handwriting.

ALICE: *(Reading)* Signed "Meryl Streep."

DEXTER: She was a famous actress during that period.

ALICE: I know who Meryl Streep was, Dexter. Please stop explaining things I already know.

DEXTER: Sorry, sorry, sorry.

ALICE: *(Reading)* "Dear Mister Gurney: I've decided to return to the stage in your marvelous play, but only if I can do it with a Buffalo accent."

DEXTER: I guess she loved to do accents.

ALICE: But is the play about Buffalo?

DEXTER: Partly. Gurney used to use Buffalo as an example of American decline and decay.

ALICE: So with these two letters, Gurney must have been walking on air.

DEXTER: Wait. *(Hands her the next document -a typewritten business letter)* This is a letter from Gerald Schoenfeld, who was a major Broadway theater-owner at that time.

ALICE: *(Reading)* "Dear Pete: I plan to produce your play immediately in the theatre I've named after myself. The piece is good enough to require an English director, and important enough for us to forego the exorbitant fees we usually charge for tickets ordered over the phone." *(To DEXTER)* Then why wasn't it produced?

DEXTER: Because the government intervened.

ALICE: How?

DEXTER: Remember how our country was desperately in debt because of the Iraq war? So at just that time the government ordered all the Broadway theatres to convert to gambling casinos.

ALICE: So Gurney's play was postponed?

DEXTER: Indefinitely.

ALICE: But still, what a play it must be! Let me read it, please!

DEXTER: *(Producing another stack of documents)* Only after you've read these.

ALICE: More preliminaries?

DEXTER: *(Handing her the first one)* They put things in perspective.

ALICE: This note is unsigned. *(Holding it up)* And it's written in a crude, illegible scrawl.

DEXTER: Give it a try.

ALICE: *(Reading slowly)* "This play...is...a...fucking piece of shit." *(To* DEXTER*)* But who...?

DEXTER: Read the letterhead.

ALICE: *(Reading)* "The Republican National Committee"

DEXTER: You see?

ALICE: But this would make me want to produce it all the more.

DEXTER: Not after you've read this. *(Displays another document)* From a conservative organization called "Focus on the Family." They tell Gurney that if he allows this play to be produced, or even mentions its existence, certain steps will be taken.

ALICE: What steps?

DEXTER: They are listed in the footnote.: *(Reading)* First: his offspring— *(Looking up)* And I assume they mean his grandchildren.... *(Reading)* would receive consistently low S A T scores all through high school. And if they played sports on weekends, they would find themselves sitting on the bench whenever their parents and grandparents came to watch.

ALICE: Now that is ultimately cruel!

DEXTER: You can see why, for the sake of his family, Gurney felt he had to withdraw his play.

ALICE: All I can say is that Gurney may have been a second-rate playwright, but he must have been a first-rate family man.

DEXTER: You'd also call him a first-rate playwright once you've read the play.

ALICE: *(Taking up the play with reverence and affection)* But it must be hopelessly out of date after all these years.

DEXTER: It's more relevant than ever.

ALICE: Then I suppose it's doomed to lie fallow until such a time when serious theatre is reborn.

DEXTER: Alice.

ALICE: What?

DEXTER: Suppose we assisted in that rebirth.

ALICE: How?

DEXTER: By putting on this play.

ALICE: Where?

DEXTER: Here. On this campus.

ALICE: In the Marvin and Mona Spellberg Memorial Auditorium?

DEXTER: Exactly.

ALICE: You remind me that the universities have always been the custodians of culture, even as civilizations have collapsed around them.

DEXTER: There you go.

ALICE: But under what auspices could we do it? The Student Drama Organization is only allowed to present scenes from the Bible and episodes from the Bush and Cheney families..

DEXTER: We'll produce it on our own. By reading it aloud to audiences, and playing all the parts ourselves.

ALICE: Just you and I?

DEXTER: Just us.

ALICE: But can you act?

DEXTER: I played Cornelius Hackle in an unauthorized production of HELLO DOLLY at a Jewish Community Center.

ALICE: Were you any good?

DEXTER: Better than Broadway. And I'm not even Jewish.

ALICE: I must say I'm tempted.

DEXTER: By me?

ALICE: By the idea of putting this thing on. In an odd way, it seems strangely appropriate. Serious drama in Gurney's time was fast dwindling to short runs with small casts and minimal scenery. We'd be right in line.

DEXTER: Then let's get at it.

ALICE: I might buy a new dress. And wear a teeny tad of make-up.

DEXTER: You'd be gilding the lily if you did, Alice.

ALICE: Oh you.

DEXTER: O K, so let's get going. As a member of the faculty, you have the right to reserve the auditorium. You could call it simply a lecture to get it by the Monitoring Committee.

ALICE: I'll call right now.

DEXTER: Great. *(Gently taking the script from her)* And while you're doing that, I'll take this script over to the copying center so you can have your own copy to rehearse with.

ALICE: That's very thoughtful.

DEXTER: One thing, though.

ALICE: What?

DEXTER: Would you allow our performance to serve as my senior thesis?

ALICE: You don't want to write anything?

DEXTER: I've been diagnosed as slightly dyslexic,
and I'm scared my writing might come out backwards,
and make my work seem reactionary.

ALICE: Dexter, you are a rascal and a sly-boots, aren't
you?

DEXTER: Faint heart ne'er won fair lady.

ALICE: Go, go, go to the copy center..

(DEXTER *goes off.*)

(ALICE *dials three digits on her phone on her desk*)

ALICE: Hello? This is Alice Tucker, in drama....
I'd like to reserve the auditorium for a dramatic
reading.... Some Saturday night would be good....
How about three weeks from now? ...Fine. That would
give me time to prepare.... Thank you.. *(She hangs up,
slides in her chair to the book case to return a book, singing
a popular show tune as she goes. Still in her chair, she begins
to kick out like a dancer)*

(Her telephone rings. She answers.)

ALICE: Yes? ...What? ...Not available? ...Could you give
me some other dates then? ... Nothing on weekends?
...How about during the week? ...How about the little
theatre then? ...Please check. I'll wait.

*(She continues to sing, now defiantly, then is interrupted on
the phone):*

ALICE: What? ...Every evening? ...How about a lecture
hall? ...All right, I'll simply take a classroom? ...Against
what rules? ...What? Nothing? Nothing at all? ...Want to
know something? I don't believe you!

(She slams down the phone as DEXTER comes back in)

ALICE: I've got bad news.

DEXTER: Me, too. You first.

ALICE: The Myron and Mona Spellberg auditorium is booked solid. And so is everything else.

DEXTER: Booked? With what?

ALICE: They said the usual stuff. Which I suppose means patriotic pep rallies. Meetings of the Scientology Club. Continuous showings of Mel Gibson's *Passion of the Christ*.

DEXTER: I don't believe that.

ALICE: Neither do I ...But what's your bad news?

DEXTER: *(Holds out his hands)* Look. No script.

ALICE: Isn't it being copied?

DEXTER: The woman at the copy center put it into the shredder by mistake.

ALICE: I don't believe that.

DEXTER: Neither do I, especially after I heard what she whispered to a co-worker.

ALICE: What did she whisper?

DEXTER: "Mission accomplished."

ALICE: Good Lord! *(Pointing to ceiling)* They've been listening in all along!

DEXTER: *(Grimly defiant)* And then notified the Copy Center.

ALICE: *(Pacing)* This is appalling, Dexter. A crucial document has been lost to history. Like one of the lost plays of Sophocles.

DEXTER: Are you ready for a recognition scene, Alice?

ALICE: All good drama has one.

DEXTER: Well here comes mine. Oh God, how dumb I've been! I recognize now I'm a loser, Alice. I totally deserve those C minuses you gave me.

ALICE: Now don't punish yourself.

DEXTER: But I've found and lost a major masterpiece.
And in the process, I suspect I've also lost you!

ALICE: Now wait. I'm thinking. *(She does.)*

DEXTER: I love it when you think, Alice.

ALICE: Didn't you say you had a good memory?

DEXTER: For baseball statistics.

ALICE: And for the specifics of Gurney's script.

DEXTER: I did say that. For example, the play begins
with a woman alone in a room—

ALICE: *(More and more passionately)* Stop! Wait! Please.
I keep telling all my students that there's nothing more
boring than simply summarizing the plot.

DEXTER: I remember that now.

ALICE: All right, then bear with me. Do you also
remember my lecture on Ibsen's HEDDA GABLER?
Or were you asleep in class?

DEXTER: Refresh my memory.

ALICE: At the end of the play, Tesman and Mrs Elvstad
get together and decide to reconstitute the manuscript,
which Hedda has so wantonly thrown into the fire.

DEXTER: It's beginning to come back.

ALICE: You and I could do the same with Gurney's
play, Dexter! We could reconstruct it, piece by piece!
You have your excellent memory and I'm an expert
on dramatic structure. Together we can at least
approximate what Gurney wrote.

DEXTER: What do we do after we've done that?

ALICE: We put it on. The way you suggested.

DEXTER: But the university blew us off.

ALICE: I'm not talking about here, Dexter, in this parochial, paranoid prison.

DEXTER: *(Wiping his cheek)* You're spitting, Alice.

ALICE: That's because I'm taking up acting again! And I want to continue my craft by performing this play out there, in the real world!

DEXTER: But where?

ALICE: Wherever the American people tend to congregate. We'll do it at Starbucks outlets and in the parking lots of Home Depot. We'll do it at NASCAR races, and along the main strip in Las Vegas. We'll do it in front of the long lines at unemployment offices, and in hospital waiting rooms where people argue about Medicare.

DEXTER: Yes! And how about in churches, synagogues, and mosques?

ALICE: Of course! *(Taking DEXTER's arm)* Theatre has always come out of religion. We'll return it to its basic beginnings! We'll make Gurney's play permanent and portable, like the Ten Commandments.

DEXTER: Or like his LOVE LETTERS.

ALICE: Never heard of it.

DEXTER: He had lovers sitting side by side reading letters.

ALICE: Sounds boring.

DEXTER: Not when the actors loved each other. Suppose we do that, too.

ALICE: Do what?

DEXTER: Become lovers.

ALICE: I haven't thought about that.

DEXTER: I have, Alice. A great deal.

ALICE: Let's cross that bridge when we come to it, Dexter. Right now, let's just go back to my apartment ... *(Shouting at the ceiling)* ...where the constitutional prohibition against unlawful search or seizure still applies—except on weekends!

DEXTER: I'm with you.

ALICE: And we'll begin to reconstitute this play.

DEXTER: Can we go to bed together first?

ALICE: No.

DEXTER: Please.

ALICE: No.

DEXTER: Oh come on.

ALICE: Maybe after we get some work done..

DEXTER: Let's do it first.

ALICE: Does it mean that much to you?

DEXTER: It does. It really does.

ALICE: Oh well. All right. *(She hurries off.)*

DEXTER: Yee Haw! *(He follows lustily.)*

(Lights change)

(Music comes up as stagehand clear ALICE's office and. set up three chairs in front of a low coffee table with a pitcher of water and three glasses on it.)

(During this, BETSY comes out, in a spot. She wears what a student would wear for an important public event. She carries a stack of index cards.)

BETSY: *(To audience)* Hi!....Welcome to the Marvin and Mona Spellberg Memorial Auditorium. My name is Betsy Baker, and I'm this year's chairperson of our new Student Lecture Committee.. *(Glances offstage)* Oh, and I'm *so* excited! Tonight, right here, on this stage, I'll be

interviewing two of the most important people in the
world! And what's so amazing, they actually met here,
not so long ago! One was a lecturer on drama , and one
was her student, and now they're married, and famous,
and they've come back to home base to share their
experiences with all of us! *(Indicating her cards)*
Naturally there has been so much interest in their visit
that we've asked people to submit their questions
ahead of time. And we've tried to select the most
appropriate ones. And here they are. *(Puts cards
carefully on the table)* O K, but before I introduce our
guests, I have to make the usual speech about cell
phones. Namely, turn them off, please, people. You
might think you already have, but we are all so used to
them now that sometimes we forget, and consequently
a cell phone can go off at just the wrong time, and ruin
the whole moment ...And now it's my great pleasure
to— *(Stops, then impulsively leaves her position by the table)*
Except I want to say this. I *hate* having to make the
cell-phone speech. It gets everything off on the wrong
foot. It makes me the cop, and you the culprits, and
we should all be on the same footing, especially tonight.
Maybe one of these days I'll no longer have to make
that speech. Maybe some day, we'll turn them off
automatically. Or not even bring them. Maybe we'll
learn not to bring them to class, either. I hear that
Professor Klein in Chemistry docks your grade if your
cell phone goes off during his lectures. You should
also know that the Athletic Department has a new rule
about them. No cell phones if you are participating in
an athletic event. Apparently some girl on the cross
country team stopped to answer her cell in the middle
of a race! And last week a cell phone went off during
a Quaker meeting in our interdenominational chapel.
Now in Quaker meetings you're supposed to be quiet
unless the Holy Spirit moves you. Well, it sure wasn't
the Holy Spirit on that cell. It was a Quaker's

room-mate looking for the remote to their T V! *(Looks up and off)* I know, I know. They're waiting. But I'm the head of the lecture committee, and I'm on a roll here. *(To audience)* Because I don't think cell phones should be allowed at meals. And I'm not just talking about the college cafeteria either. I mean restaurants, too. And in your own home. A meal is a sacred thing. Professor Kibel in Literature says that when we break bread together we remind ourselves of our common nature. He read us that part in *The Iliad* when Priam, the doomed old King of Troy, comes to beg Achilles for the body of his son Hector, whom Achilles has killed and dragged around the city walls. So Priam begs for the body, and Achilles gives it up, and then what happens? They sit down together and share a leg of lamb! The father and the murderer of his son! It's extremely moving. *(She gets teary.)* It says that life must go on, even after a situation like that! So when people start chattering on their cell phones while they eat, they're saying that something more important than the meal is going on somewhere else, which is wrong, because eating together is the heart of the matter. So no phones at meals, please. We should make that a rule. *(A slight pause only)* And I don't think we should use cell phones when we're walking down the street, either. Why? Because when we're walking places, we should be noticing our surroundings, and greeting people we know, and how can we do that if we're jabbering away on our cells. That means we're out of it, we're elsewhere, and so we bump into people. Or ignore them, which is worse. One time I was walking through the Student Union plaza, and everyone there was either talking on cell-phones or listening to their I-pods. No one was noticing anyone else. It was like being in some zombie movie like THE DAWN OF THE DEAD. I wanted to shout out, "Hey, look! I'm here, I'm alive, I'm a human being!" I was so upset when I got to

philosophy class that I mentioned this to my teacher,
and you know what she said? She said that cell phones
are undermining our sense of what the Greeks
called the *polis*, which is the basic building block
of democracy. She said we need to remind ourselves
constantly of our common interconnectedness. That's
why we have the agora, or the piazza, or the village
square, or Main Street, or right here, in this theatre,
and if we lose all that, democracy goes out the window.
So we've got to make rules here. We've got to restrict
cell-phones. As we did with spitting. Or cigarettes.
Because we're really talking about civility here. That's
what we're really talking about. O K? O K. *(Returns to
stand by her table)* And now it is my great pleasure to
introduce a man and a woman who began their journey
to world-wide acclaim right here at this very university,
and who need no introduction beyond that. May we
welcome, please...well, they've asked that we call them
simply Alice and Dexter!

*(BETSY encourages applause as. DEXTER and ALICE enter
graciously and theatrically, hand in hand, waving to the
audience. ALICE wears a glamorous evening dress and
DEXTER a Hollywood-style tux. They take a couple of
theatrical bows. The chatter here is lively and fast.)*

BETSY: I apologize for my spiel about cell-phones.
I got carried away.

ALICE: No, no. That's fine. That's good

DEXTER: Freedom of speech and all that.

ALICE: Besides, it gave me time to fix my hair.

DEXTER: Thank God for the mirror backstage.

ALICE: Dexter had forgotten to zip up his fly.

DEXTER: Story of my life.

ALICE: You can say that again.

DEXTER: But I won't.

BETSY: I felt weird using your first names.

DEXTER: Not at all. Our contract insists on it, wherever we go.

BETSY: But you're such celebrities, all over the world! Using your first names sounds so...chummy.

DEXTER: We never use our last name.

ALICE: With last names, you drag around a lot of extra baggage .

DEXTER: Ethnic identities, spousal commitments, all that stuff.

ALICE: We like to factor that out. We don't like titles either.

DEXTER: Alice has her PhD now.

ALICE: But don't you dare call me Doctor.

DEXTER: Technically I'm a Doctor, too, because we've got these honorary degrees.

ALICE: But we said no to all that.

DEXTER: We don't even like being called mother and father...

ALICE: Our children call us Dexter and Alice.

DEXTER: It keeps us all on the same team.

BETSY: Wow. Children! I keep forgetting you have children.

ALICE: That's just as well.

DEXTER: We keep them out of the spotlight.

ALICE: Never talk about them.

DEXTER: Never.

ALICE: There's nothing more boring than people talking about their children.

DEXTER: It starts other people talking about theirs.

ALICE: And the people who don't have any get left out. And they're the ones with more interesting things to say.

BETSY: How many do you have?

DEXTER: Children? *(To* ALICE*)* Shall we tell them? *(To* BETSY*)* It's embarrassing.

ALICE: Oh why the hell not? People can always look it up in Who's Who.

DEXTER: We have five children..

ALICE: *(To audience)* Within seven and half years! It's disgusting.

DEXTER: Then we discovered what was causing it.

ALICE: He thinks that's funnier than I do.

(Genial laughter)

BETSY: Um. Maybe we should get down to business.

ALICE: Yes, exactly. Enough of this bedroom badinage.

BETSY: *(Indicating the chairs)* You asked for a Q and A . So I'll Q and you A.

DEXTER: Fine.

BETSY: So please sit.

DEXTER: O K. We'll sit. ...But at events like this, we like to stand up occasionally.

ALICE: *(Posing, finding her light)* Or walk around. To make a point, or something,

BETSY: Feel free.

ALICE: Thank you. Because that's what we want, isn't it? To feel free..

DEXTER: And that's what we didn't feel not too long ago, if you remember.

BETSY: You mean the Bush thing?

ALICE: It certainly started with Bush.

DEXTER: We like to say it was when Bush came to shove.

ALICE: He used to get a laugh on that line.

(DEXTER *brushes off* ALICE's *chair with his tux handkerchief. Theyt close together, and nudge and nuzzle and get a big kick out of each other as they answer the questions.*)

BETSY: Shall we move on? (*Picking up the sack of question cards*) These questions were selected from a huge number submitted ahead of time.

ALICE: I hope you omitted the hostile ones.

BETSY: Oh, there were very few of those.

DEXTER: What? No Republicans left in this part of the world?

BETSY: No hostile Republicans, anyway.

ALICE: Let's hope they're extinct—like the dodo or the passenger pigeon.

DEXTER: I'll bet the moderate ones are bouncing back, like the wild turkey.

BETSY: So. First question? (*Taking first paper from folder, looking at it*) Ah. The Nobel Prize thing.

DEXTER: Uh-oh. (*To audience*) Alice and I disagree about this one.

ALICE: Disagree mightily.

BETSY: Want to skip it?

ALICE: No, let's deal with it head-on.

BETSY: O K. *(Reading from paper)* This questioner wants to know, "Why did you refuse to accept the Nobel Prize for Literature?"

DEXTER: The answer to that is only one of us refused.

ALICE: I refused.

BETSY: Would you explain why?

ALICE: Gladly. For the umpteenth time. *(To audience)* I refused the Nobel Prize for the play POST MORTEM because, no matter how good the play is, and no matter how enthusiastically it has been received all over the world, the fact remains that I didn't write it. And neither did Dexter.

DEXTER: Here's where we disagree.

ALICE: Gurney wrote it.

DEXTER: We *virtually* wrote it. We reconstituted the whole thing.. From scratch.

ALICE: What we did was *reassemble* the play, from Dexter's memory and my sense of theatre. To accept the Nobel for what amounted to a reconstruction would be hubristic.

DEXTER: Dig that "Hubristic." *(To audience)* It means full of overweening pride.

ALICE: They know what it means.

DEXTER: They do now, because I told them.

ALICE: And I told you.

DEXTER: True. *(To audience)* Isn't she great?

ALICE: *(To BETSY)* Next question?

BETSY: *(Searching through several questions)* Here's a follow-up. This concerns the recent article.

DEXTER: Which recent article? The profile in *The New Yorker*? Or the one in *Sports Illustrated* on my golf game?

BETSY: The cover article in *Time*.

DEXTER: Oh right.

ALICE: Isn't it wonderful how *Time* magazine has gone back to the way it was. It is now serious and substantial.

BETSY: *(To audience)* For those who haven't yet had a chance to read it, the *Time* article says that there are certain literary works, like Harriet Beecher Stowe's UNCLE TOM's CABIN or A R Gurney's POST MORTEM, which have had a major effect on American history. Stowe sounded the death knell for slavery. Gurney is responsible for the major changes that have occurred recently in our country and in the world.

DEXTER: I'll say this. Gurney certainly is responsible for a major change in *me*. *(To audience)* When I was a student here, I used Gurney's play as a way of getting Alice into bed.

ALICE: Easy now.

DEXTER: But now I've learned to love the play.

ALICE: *(Embraces him)* That's sweet, darling.

DEXTER: But that doesn't mean I neglect my conjugal responsibilities.

ALICE: You've made your point, darling.

BETSY: *Time* also says that because of the play, the American people are now once again welcomed and celebrated wherever they go..

ALICE: Oh well

DEXTER: No, it's true. When we performed in Iran, the audience wouldn't stop cheering.

ALICE: The English still have some problems with us.

DEXTER: They don't like most American plays.

ALICE: I suppose it's because they see themselves as the custodians of theatre.

DEXTER: They like to call the shots. And they like more scenery.

BETSY: *(Taking a paper out of the folder)* Now for the next question... *(Reads it)* Oh I don't know. Maybe we'll skip this one. *(Puts it back)*

DEXTER: Why?

BETSY: It seems a little ... trivial.

ALICE: Trivial?

BETSY: Unimportant.

ALICE: You never know. Sometimes the Devil is in the details.

DEXTER: Sock it to us.

BETSY: O K, we needn't spend much time on it. *(Reading the question)* Someone wants to know if you ever found out who killed Gurney?

ALICE: Oh that. *(To* DEXTER*)* Shall we go there?

DEXTER: Why the hell not?

ALICE: Actually, it's a little complicated. Do we know who killed Gurney? The answer is yes and no.

DEXTER: We have to talk about Dick Cheney.

BETSY: Are you saying Cheney killed Gurney.

ALICE: I'm saying yes and no. *(To* DEXTER*)* Take it from there.

DEXTER: Gladly.

BETSY: Wait. *(To audience)* Let me make it clear to the now-legal immigrants. *Ricardo Cheney fue el Vice Presidente para Jorge W Bush.*

ALICE: Or "Poquito Bush", as the history books now call him

DEXTER: And Cheney is attacked in Gurney's play.

ALICE: You should talk about the note.

DEXTER: Oh right. That. The note.

BETSY: What note?

DEXTER: There was a note found among Cheney's papers after he died.

BETSY: Saying what?

DEXTER: Saying "Get Gurney."

BETSY: Get Gurney?

DEXTER: Which sounds like an order Cheney wrote to one of his hit men.

BETSY: Get Gurney.

DEXTER: Right. Because of what Gurney wrote about him in the play.

ALICE: But there's a problem with that.

BETSY: A problem?

ALICE: The problem is that the note was written on hospital stationery. Which indicates that Cheney was in the hospital at the time he wrote it.

BETSY: For his heart?

ALICE: For his hemorrhoids.

BETSY: Oh.

ALICE: And it's common knowledge that he was unhappy with his room. So some people argue that it was simply a note to the nurse saying "Get gurney".

DEXTER: They say it looked like a small "g".

ALICE: Which means Cheney simply wanted a gurney to be wheeled to a better room.

DEXTER: Do you buy that? I'm not sure I buy it.

ALICE: The Cheney family buys it.

DEXTER: Well sure. Obviously. Which brings us back to the play. Where Cheney is a major bad guy.

ALICE: The English wanted to cut him out, you know.

DEXTER: Cut out Cheney?

ALICE: The National Theatre called this morning. They were willing to do their own production of POST MORTEM if they could cut the Cheney scenes.

DEXTER: Why?

ALICE: They said the character was dated and unimportant.

DEXTER: So what did you say?

ALICE: I told them I'd been doing some thinking about the play, and saw a tragic dimension in Dick Cheney. He takes on some of the majestic characteristics of Milton's Satan, in *Paradise Lost*.

DEXTER: Wow!

ALICE: In fact, when he retires to his ranch in Wyoming, Gurney compares him to a major nemesis in English history, the exiled Napoleon on the island of Saint Helena.

DEXTER: But does that make him tragic?

ALICE: Of course. When his daughter comes to visit him, in a scene that reminds us of King Lear and Cordelia, they talk about how the world has fallen apart since he took office. And for a moment we think, uh-oh, here we go, Gurney is going to give us some corny recognition scene where Cheney apologizes for what he's done.

(BETSY *raises her hand, like a student in class.* ALICE *gives her a nod.)*

BETSY: But when his daughter asks him if he has some regrets...

DEXTER: He just says no..

BETSY: And when she asks if he would do the same thing all over again.

DEXTER: He just says yes.

ALICE: Exactly! So his daughter asks, How do you live with yourself, Daddy? How do you justify the terrible damage you've done, all over the world?

DEXTER: And Cheney says ...

ALL THREE: *(Together)* Mistakes were made.

ALICE: That's all he says.

BETSY: Mistakes were made.

ALICE: *(To audience)* Which is a quote from Richard M Nixon.

DEXTER: After Watergate. "Mistakes were made."
(To ALICE*)* And you told Brits that was tragic?

ALICE: I did. We expect Cheney to apologize, or fall on his sword, or *some*thing, but no. I told the Brits that Gurney goes *beyond* Shakespeare in having his character incapable of recognizing his own responsibility. He is locked into his own unassailable pride, like one of those majestic sinners in Dante's *Inferno*, who unwittingly provide their own punishment

DEXTER: Beautiful!

ALICE: .So that's what I meant when I told the Brits that in Gurney's play Cheney acquires a profoundly tragic dimension.

DEXTER: And the Brits bought it?

ALICE: Absolutely. They now plan to produce the play, and bring it over next spring in time for the Tony awards.

DEXTER: *(To audience)* And that's what I call good teaching! Live and learn. Or should I say love and learn!

BETSY: But did Cheney kill Gurney?

ALICE: Ah. That brings us back to Yes and No.

DEXTER: *(To ALICE)* Shall we take the next step?

ALICE: I think we have to.

DEXTER: I'll get Exhibit A.

ALICE: It won't solve everything,, but get it anyway. It's in my tote bag in my dressing room.

DEXTER: *(Getting up)* Exhibit A coming up. *(He goes off.)*

ALICE: *(To BETSY)* You must have heard that after Dexter discovered the original script of POST MORTEM, it was shredded by this university in the name of national security.

BETSY: Oh yes. And I believe the university ultimately had to apologize to its alumni.

ALICE: Still the legacy of that terrible period lingered on. So now we have to talk about another scene.

BETSY: Another scene in the play?

ALICE: No this time, we turn to a scene in life, dear girl.

BETSY: Life? I love life.

ALICE: *(Looks off)* And here comes Dexter, like a Greek messenger, bearing a piece of evidence.

(DEXTER *returns, carrying a script*)

DEXTER: *(Showing it to the audience)* Exhibit A on display.

ALICE: *(Taking script; showing it to audience)* This is the script Dexter was using when we were first starting out.

DEXTER: We were rehearsing in an abandoned General Motors showroom.

ALICE: Act it out, darling. Show, don't tell.

DEXTER: O K. We were rehearsing a scene, and I was holding my script like this. *(Holds it close to his chest)*

ALICE: I was standing across from him, like this.

DEXTER: And I was delivering my line about how it was high time we changed the world.

ALICE: When suddenly a shot rang out from behind an old, unsold Buick.

DEXTER: *(Acting it out)* And I crumpled to the floor, like this ...

ALICE: I thought he'd been killed! I ran to him. And held up his head. *(She does)*

DEXTER: *(Holding up his head)* But I was fine. *(Getting up)* I had just had the wind knocked out of me. *(Displaying the script)* Because the bullet had hit this script instead of me.. *(Showing the hole in the cover)* Notice the bullet hole.

ALICE: Show them how far the bullet got, darling.

DEXTER: *(Poking his finger through the hole)* See? It came to a stop here. At page one hundred and seventy-three!

ALICE: The play at that time was a little too long.

DEXTER: Thank the Lord. Otherwise I'd be dead.

ALICE: Since then, we've done some serious cutting.

DEXTER: Otherwise the audience would be dead.

(Genial laughter)

BETSY: But does that shot have anything to do with Vice President Cheney?

ALICE: Once again, the answer is yes and no.
(To DEXTER*)* Tell her, darling.

DEXTER: O.K. After the shooting, a passing policeman stopped an old, rust-encrusted Hummer which was lumbering away from the scene. The cop noticed the smoking gun, extricated the driver and wrestled him the ground.

ALICE: It turns out the man's name was Yenehc.

BETSY: Yenehc?.

DEXTER: Y-E-N-E-H-C. Yenehc..

BETSY: Was he a disgruntled Serbian nationalist?

ALICE: He was not.

DEXTER: You may have heard through the grapevine that I suffer from dyslexia.

ALICE: That's one of the reasons he had such trouble in my drama courses.

DEXTER: The point is, when he gave his name, I automatically spelled it backwards in my mind. It came out...guess what?

BETSY: *(Working it out)* Y-E-N-E- H-C... Hmmm... C-H-E-N-E-Y? ...Cheney!

DEXTER: Exactly! It turned out he was Dick Cheney's grand-nephew. To save embarrassment, he had changed his name after Cheney fell into disrepute.

ALICE: But he was trying to revenge his great-uncle's reputation.

DEXTER: The police tried to questioned him..

ALICE: But like his great uncle, in front of his draft board, he kept saying he had other priorities.

BETSY: What other priorities?

ALICE: He was scheduled for a sex-change operation.

DEXTER: So we decided not to press charges.

BETSY: What?

ALICE: In fact, we encouraged him to go through with his operation..

DEXTER: We even contributed financially to it.

BETSY: Why?

ALICE: Because we believe that most of the trouble in this world is caused by people who find themselves playing the wrong part. George W Bush is a prime example. Or Cheney. Or this poor lout. Only this one had the good sense to recast himself in a different role.

DEXTER: So the operation worked!

ALICE: Worked beautifully. Made him...or rather her... a different person. She returned to her original family name. She now calls herself Chandra Cheney and works at a Day Care Center in the inner city.

DEXTER: And she's no longer brooding or sour or secretive, like her great uncle.

ALICE: In fact, we invited her over for a drink,

BETSY: And she came?

ALICE: She came, and behaved like a regular pussy cat. She told us that the problem for the Cheney family had always been an excess of testosterone. All that growling and chest thumping and playing with guns.

DEXTER: She felt that her operation had put a stop to that, once and for all. So after our second drink, I finally asked her point-blank: "Hey Chandra, baby," I said.

"Tell us the truth. Did your great uncle Dick Cheney
kill, or order to be killed, the playwright Pete Gurney?"

ALICE: And guess what her answer to that was?

BETSY: Yes and no?

ALICE: Exactly! Yes and no.

BETSY: So will the answer always be yes and no?

ALICE: Maybe not There's a group of scholars at the
University of Michigan who have recently come up
with a totally different theory on who killed Gurney.

BETSY: Who?

DEXTER: Barbara Bush.

ALICE: But let's not go there.

DEXTER: Right. Let's not.

ALICE: As you can see, who killed Gurney is a very
complicated question.

BETSY: Oh you guys, you guys, you're so totally terrific!
(To audience) Aren't they marvelous? Isn't it fabulous
how they give Cheney and Barbara Bush and everyone
else in the world the benefit of the doubt?

ALICE: Well, we try.

BETSY: But may we now move on?

ALICE: Absolutely. The play's the thing, after all,
in spite of the passing of the playwright. Life is short,
but art is long.

BETSY: This is so awesome. *(To audience)* Isn't this
awesome? Just being in the same room with these folks?
Hearing them tell us how it is. *(Shuffling through the
cardsr)* There are so many wonderful questions here
for them to answer. *(Suddenly puts the cards down, leaves
her chair)* Except I'm not going to ask them.

ALICE: No more questions?

BETSY: Remember earlier how I went off on a tangent with my talk about cell phones.

DEXTER: *(Dryly)* Vaguely

BETSY: Well I do that a lot. I go off on tangents. In fact, now I want to go off on another one. I want to ask you to perform a scene from your play.

DEXTER: Which scene?

BETSY: The love scene from Act Two.

DEXTER: Oh boy.

ALICE: Oh no.

BETSY: Oh please, Alice. Because it all boils down to love in the end, doesn't it?

DEXTER: It sure does.

BETSY: So do the scene. You don't have to get up and move around You don't even have to make faces and gestures. *(She begins to slide the table to one side and rearrange the chairs.)*

ALICE: We didn't bring our scripts.

BETSY: Then you could work from the published version. I'll bet half the people in this audience have brought along their own copies of POST MORTEM for the book-signing afterwards. *(To audience)* The New York Review of Books said that this scene, with the exception of the balcony scene in ROMEO AND JULIET, may well be the most glorious love scene ever written for the stage.

DEXTER: "May well be"? It goddam well is.

ALICE: Too glorious, maybe.

BETSY: Why do you say that?

ALICE: Because not so long ago, Dexter and I were dumb enough to do that love scene at a charity event.

BETSY: Out of context?

ALICE: Out of context.

BETSY: Wow!

ALICE: And, to add insult to injury, we'd both had a glass or two of white wine before we did it.

DEXTER: Which is maybe *why* we did it.

ALICE: The point is you should never drink before going on stage. Never. That is a rule.

DEXTER: The point is, we really got into that love scene. We took off in that scene! We flew!

ALICE: Too much so, I'm afraid.

BETSY: Did you...I mean, did you...I mean, on *stage?*

ALICE: Nonsense. I'm referring to what it led to in the audience. *(She indicates it caused an orgy)*

DEXTER: I'll tell you what it led to. It led to a run on the morning-after pill the next day!

ALICE: Which thank God was by then readily available over the counter.

BETSY: *(To audience)* There was an article in *The Economist* which argued that the second-act love scene in the play POST MORTEM is directly responsible for the decline in the divorce rate in every state except California.

ALICE: I think that's over-stating the case, Betsy. I really do.

BETSY: So how about it?

DEXTER: I hate to sound crass, Betsy, but we normally get paid to perform. We get paid more than this university could possibly afford.

BETSY: But this is your old stomping ground. Many of your old classmates and students have come specially to see you. Couldn't you give us just a teeny little freebie? Puh-leeze.

DEXTER: *(To* ALICE*)* We could do just the first section.

ALICE: No.

DEXTER: Just up to the tricky part.

ALICE: I said No!

DEXTER: O K, O K, O K. *(To* BETSY*)* No means no, in our household..

BETSY: Because of what it does to the audience?

ALICE: Because of what it does to me.

DEXTER: This is something recent..

ALICE: *(Carefully)* Recent. And different.

(Pause)

DEXTER: *(To* ALICE*)* Maybe we should say more. We can't just leave things hanging like this.

ALICE: Why can't we?

DEXTER: What? You're the big expert on theatre, and I need to tell you why? Because you can't just set up a scene , and then walk away from it, that's why. You're always saying that good drama is expectations fulfilled.

(Another pause)

ALICE: I've never spoken about this before.

DEXTER: Except to me.

ALICE: *(To audience)* Yes, but he doesn't really get it.

DEXTER: That's true, I don't.

BETSY: *(Indicating the audience)* But maybe *we'll* get it if you tell us.

(ALICE *looks at the audience)*

ALICE: All right. *(To* DEXTER*)* Tell them.

DEXTER: How can I tell them if I don't get it?

ALICE: You get it enough to give them some idea.

DEXTER: You tell them

ALICE: I could try, but you know what would happen.

DEXTER: Right. O K. *(Comes downstage; to audience)* Alice doesn't like the play any more.

ALICE: That's not true!

DEXTER: Doesn't like doing it, then.

BETSY: Not even the love scene?

DEXTER: Especially not the love scene.

BETSY: But you do the play all over the world.

DEXTER: Not any more.

BETSY: But we keep reading about it being done.

DEXTER: Other people do it now. Movie stars and candidates for political office.

ALICE: *(To* DEXTER*)* And you do it, too. Admit it.

DEXTER: Yes I do it. Occasionally. With other women.

ALICE: Any chance he gets.

DEXTER: But it's never the same as doing it with you. *(He returns to stand behind her)*

ALICE: Thank you, sweetheart.

BETSY: Why won't you do it, Alice?

DEXTER: She won't do it because she can't.

BETSY: Can't?

DEXTER: Because whenever she does it, she breaks down and cries.

BETSY: The play makes her cry?

DEXTER: Every time.

BETSY: Even the love scene?

DEXTER: The love scene most of all.

BETSY: Is that true, Alice?

(ALICE *nods, on the verge of tears*)

BETSY: Why does it make you cry, Alice?

DEXTER: She'd cry if she told you. .

BETSY: *(To* DEXTER*)* Could you tell us, then?

DEXTER: No. Because, as she said, I don't really understand it.

(Pause)

BETSY: *(Crossing to the table; picking up the question cards)* Maybe we should just go back to the Q and A.

ALICE: We can't go back.

DEXTER: You can never go back in the theater. You've got to keep moving forward.

ALICE: *(Tearfully, hugging him))* See? He's learned so much...O K. I'll try to explain. *(She comes downstage, takes a deep breath)*

(A cell phone rings in the back of the audience.)

BETSY: Wouldn't you know! *(Calling out)* Turn that fucking thing off!

(The cell phone stops ringing)

BETSY: I could strangle that person!.

ALICE: No, no, Betsy. Civility, remember. *(Out to audience, shading her eyes)* Dear Sir or Madam—whichever you are. When you get home tonight, I want you to pick up your cell phone carefully between your thumb and forefinger, and hold it away from your body, and take it out-of-doors, and seek a secluded spot of soil, and dig a small hole. Then I want you to drop the device in, and systematically drive a stake through its heart.

DEXTER: Isn't she the best?

BETSY: But can we go on?

ALICE: Oh yes. We have to.

BETSY: You were talking about crying.

(Leading ALICE back to her chair; DEXTER sits in his chair which is now off to one side.)

ALICE: Yes. I was saying that I sometimes cry—and may do so again—because A R Gurney has given the world this big, broad, beautiful play which has brought about peace among nations, and universal health care, and convenient public transportation, and an equitable tax system, *but... (She almost cries again.)*

BETSY: But what, Alice?

ALICE: He never tells us how to live. It's as if he's arranged for this big, beautiful party, with flowers all around, and happy waiters, and deliciously healthy food set up at the buffet table, and an orchestra all tuned up, with everyone invited and raring to go, but he doesn't tell us what we're supposed to do when we get there.

DEXTER: We're supposed to enjoy ourselves, darling.

ALICE: Yes, but how?

DEXTER: We're supposed to talk, dance, make love.

ALICE: But how? And why? What for? When we talk, what are we supposed to say? When the band strikes up, what kind of music should it play? You see? We don't know. Gurney sets everything up, but he never tell us how to live.

DEXTER: Sweetheart...darling...

ALICE: No, I'm sorry, but I take this very personally.

(BETSY *backs away from her.* DEXTER *stays in his seat)*

ALICE: *(To audience)* A while ago, Dexter and I fell in love and had a wonderful time in bed, and produced all these wonderful children. But now they're here, what should we be teaching them? Should we let them see these horrible movies where people swear and blow up automobiles and kill each other? Are video games any better? Or even public television? Is Harvard really the key to salvation, or is it better to enroll in the school of hard knocks? Is a high paying job the end of the rainbow? Or is it better to be happy in our work? What's good, what's bad? This play has no moral center.

DEXTER: *(Standing at his chair)* It has those speeches about being fair, darling. It has those great speeches about everyone in the world having enough money live on.

ALICE: *(Going to him)* Oh yes? Is that it? Is money the answer? I don't see it. I don't see how money makes that much difference, except to fly Business Class, and for most people those seats are always blacked out anyway. No, no. It's not enough just to live. How do you live well?

BETSY: Have you tried Prozac or Zoloft?

DEXTER: They don't help

ALICE: I keep thinking about poor Mister Gurney— who was no spring chicken when he wrote this

thing—scribbling away, finally coming up with POST
MORTEM at the end of his career, and being unable
to give it any kind of a moral center. And because it
doesn't have one, it leaves the lasting impression that
he was just fooling around.

DEXTER: Oh darling, no. It's a major work and it will
last as long as civilization does.

ALICE: But civilizations *don't* last. And most of the plays
they produce die with them. This one came out of a
particular political situation, and I'll give it only a year
or two more at the most before it seems as dated as
Uncle Tom's Cabin. Because by then, other systems of
government will have grown up like weeds in the
rubble of this one, and other Dick Cheneys will emerge
from the ruins with all the problems they bring with
them. (*Again she is on the verge of tears.*)

BETSY: Then someone will write something else to set
those things straight.

ALICE: Oh yes? So the best we can hope for is endless
cycles of misbehavior and corruption and ineffectual
reform, with no real moral center to pull it all together.
Unless...

DEXTER: Unless what, darling?

ALICE: Oh skip it.

BETSY: No. Unless what?

ALICE: I remember once I had this Sunday school
teacher who told us how things were before the birth
of Christ. The Romans had established a comparatively
peaceful world, with a legal system that was quite fair,
and good roads, and the right for Roman citizens to
travel anywhere and do pretty much what they wanted.
And all along the way they could stop at theatres and
amphitheatres to enjoy various entertainments, and
there were plenty of different gods to choose from,

along with an atmosphere of tolerance that went with them. But underneath all that activity, my Sunday school teacher said, there was a kind of permanent ache. The whole world sort of lay there, worn out and exhausted, and deep in their souls, people yearned for something new and special to happen. And by God it did.

DEXTER: Christianity happened.

ALICE: That's it. Christianity happened. *(Goes to him again)* And Saint Paul's Epistle to the Romans became the first moment of real warmth in Western literature since Plato's account of the death of Socrates, four hundred years before.

DEXTER: *(To audience)* Isn't she amazing?

ALICE: And Christianity went on to promise a better life. At least in the world beyond. And it proposed specific ways of behaving if you wanted to get there.

BETSY: Oh no. Are you saying we have to go through Christianity again?

DEXTER: No, no. She's just saying we need more religion in our lives.

ALICE: I'm not even saying that. *(To audience)* The dear man keeps getting it wrong. *(To DEXTER)* More religion could lead to another Bush. Or another Bin Laden.

DEXTER: Gotcha.

ALICE: So I'm just saying we have this need for some mutual sense of justice, some universally accepted common ground. So when people do harm, they can't simply say, "Mistakes were made." They'll have to say, "I broke a natural law. I apologize to my fellow human being. Now how do I make amends?"

BETSY: Wouldn't that be wonderful?

ALICE: Because if we don't have that common understanding, something worse might show up the next time around. Some rough beast might slouch toward Bethlehem to be born.

BETSY: Hey! We studied that poem in English! It was written by William Butler Yeets.

ALICE: It's pronounced Yates, dear.

BETSY: Whatever.

ALICE: So where do we find some hint of a moral universe, or at least some basic sense of civility? *(To* BETSY*)* Which you talked about yourself in your speech on cell-phones.

BETSY: Did I do that?

ALICE: You did, Betsy. And I commend you for it.

BETSY: Much good it did. A cell phone just went off. Oh, this is all suddenly very depressing. *(Indicating audience)* Can't you say something more positive for people to take home with them?

ALICE: Oh sure. I can still do that. *(Puts her arm around* BETSY, *and this time does this speech straight, with no Southern accent)* "...Maybe we are a long way frombeing made in God's image, but Betsy—my sister—there has been *some* progress since then! Such things as art—as poetry and music—such kinds of new light have come into the world... In some kinds of people some tenderer feelings have had some little beginning! That we have got to make *grow*! And *cling* to, and hold as our flag! In this dark march toward whatever it is we're approaching... *Don't hang back with the brutes!*"

DEXTER: *(To audience)* We're back where we started. With Tennessee Williams.

ALICE: We certainly haven't gotten much farther.

BETSY: Could I add something?

ALICE: Of course you can.

BETSY: I just think the fact that... *(Turning to the audience)* ...these *people* are here, when there are so many other more convenient or comforting or cheaper things they could easily have done.

DEXTER: Right. Like sitting around, watching T V or renting a D V D, or going to a Red Sox game..

BETSY: Exactly, but they didn't do that. They got up, and got out, and came here, and paid money, and sat through some long speeches, and that in itself says something, doesn't it? It says we all have some basic need to come together and think about these things. If it says nothing else, doesn't it at least say that? And isn't that a start, Alice? Can't we all take that home with us, Alice? Can't we?

(Pause)

DEXTER: Betsy's asking you a question, darling. What do you say to that?

ALICE: What do I say? I'll tell you what I say. I say thank you. And good night. *(She goes out quickly.)*

BETSY: I was hoping she'd say more...

DEXTER: That's what she always says at the end of POST MORTEM.

BETSY: Just "thank you and good night"?

DEXTER: *(Nodding)* It's the last line of the play. *(Picks up the script which has been left on the table)* She always ends with that. And then I always follow by saying the same thing. *(Bowing to audience)* "Thank you and good night." *(And he goes, carrying the script with him.)*

(BETSY is left alone on stage.)

BETSY: But there are so many more questions we haven't talked about! There's one about racism.... And another about the abortion issue... There's so much more here we need to talk about! ...Oh well. Maybe we've talked enough. Thank you and good night. *(She hurries off.)*

(Curtain)

END OF PLAY